LET'S BAKE

◆ ◆ ◆ ◆ ◆

Dr. Oetker

Sterling Publishing Co., Inc.   New York

Library of Congress Cataloging-in-Publication Data

Kinder Backbuch. English.
    Let's bake / Dr. Oetker ; [translated by Annette Englander].
        p.   cm.
    Translation of: Kinder Backbuch.
    Includes index.
    Summary: Presents baking recipes for choco-orange cupcakes,
marzipan lucky charms, and other sweet treats.
    ISBN 0-8069-8534-8
    1. Baking—Juvenile literature.   [1. Baking.   2. Cookery.]
I. Englander, Annette.   II. Dr. Oetker (Firm).   III. Title.
TX765.K5313   1992
641.7′1—dc20   91-45595
                                                                      CIP
                                                                       AC

Translated by Annette Englander

English translation © 1992 by Sterling Publishing Company
387 Park Avenue South, New York, N.Y. 10016
Original edition published under the title
Kinder Backbuch © 1990 by Ceres Verlag and
Rudolf-August-Oetker KG, Bielefeld
Spencer characters © 1990 by Debertin, licensed through
Agentur für Urheberrechtliche Merchandising München KG
Distributed in Canada by Sterling Publishing
% Canadian Manda Group, P.O. Box 920, Station U
Toronto, Ontario, Canada M8Z 5P9
Distributed in Great Britain and Europe by Cassell PLC
Villiers House, 41/47 Strand, London WC2N 5JE
Distributed in Australia by Capricorn Link Ltd.
P.O. Box 665, Lane Cove, NSW 2066
Printed in Hong Kong

10 9 8 7 6 5 4 3 2 1

Sterling ISBN   0-8069-8534-8

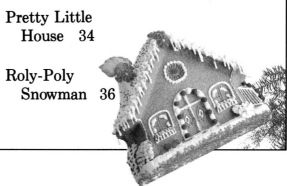
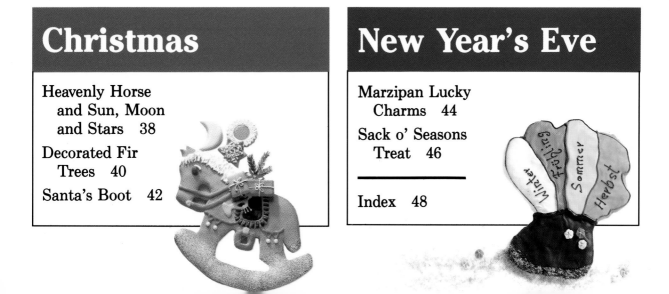

A Note to the Reader

Learning to cook can be challenging and fun. This book is intended to provide many opportunities for both, as well as the satisfaction that comes from preparing a treat the whole family can enjoy.

It is, however, strongly recommended that a responsible adult stand by, whenever a young person is using this book, to answer questions and provide help—especially with the proper use of the stove and in handling hot foods which can pose dangers.

Before beginning, here are a few good cooking-procedure "rules" to follow:

- Always wash your hands before working with food
- Wear an apron to protect your clothing
- Read the recipe you are going to prepare carefully all the way through
- Make sure you have all the measured ingredients and utensils you will need to complete the recipe on hand

- Pre-heat the oven
- Use oven mitts or pot holders when handling hot foods
- While learning, don't be afraid to ask for help

That said, grab a mixing bowl and a wooden spoon and **Let's Bake!**

Measurements

Abbreviations used:

Common

oz = ounce
pkg = package
t = teaspoon
T = tablespoon

Metric

cm = centimetre
g = gram
L = litre
mL = millilitre

Baking Needs

Here are some of the things you will need in order to make the cookies, cakes, and tasty-treat recipes in this book:

1. Mixing bowl
2. Sieve
3. Wooden spoon
4. Wooden spoon
5. Brush
6. Kneading hooks (for mixer)
7. Electric mixer
8. Small bowl
9. Rolling pin

10. Semi-circle muffin tin
11. Kitchen knife
12. Toothpicks
13. Wax paper
14. Garlic press
15. Pastry scraper
16. Sifter
17. Construction paper
18. Scissors
19. Pencil
20. Transparent tape
21. Tablespoon
22. Cookie cutters
23. Pastry bag and nozzles
24. Pots with handles
    (2 sizes)
25. Water glass
26. Lamb tin
27. Parchment paper
28. Wire whisk
29. Rubber scraper
30. Cake rack

Funny Faces

(10 portions)

What You Need

For the Dough

2 extra-large egg whites
½ cup sugar (125 g)
¼ t vanilla flavoring
1 cup all-purpose flour
   (125 g)
2 T cornstarch (30 g)
½ t baking powder
2 extra-large egg yolks

For the Filling

4 oz nutted fudge or nougat
   (125 g)
   or
1 cup prepared pudding,
   vanilla
7 T butter, softened (100 g)

For the Garnish

6½ oz white marzipan paste
   (200 g)
¾ cup confectioners' sugar
   (125 g)
food coloring

For the Icing

¾ cup confectioners' sugar
   (125 g)
2 T lemon juice
decorating gel

How It's Done

1. Place parchment paper on the baking sheet. Use a small glass to draw circles about 2½ inches (6 cm) in diameter on the paper.

2. *For the dough,* whip the egg white with an electric mixer. Add the sugar slowly and mix in. Stop and scrape the sides of the bowl when needed. Continue to beat until the mixture is very stiff.

3. Remove the whipped egg white from mixer. Add the vanilla flavoring and mix it in slowly.

4. Combine the flour with the cornstarch and baking powder. Sift it onto the stiff egg-white mixture.

5. Add the egg yolk and carefully fold everything together.

6. Spoon the batter into a pastry bag with just a hole

at the tip. Squeeze the batter into the middle of each of the drawn circles to fill them.

7. Slide the baking sheet into the *pre-heated* oven. Bake the dough circles until they are light brown.

Oven setting:
400°F (200°C)

Baking time:
10–12 minutes

8. Lift the baked circles off the paper with a spatula. Put them on a cake rack to cool.

9. *For chocolate filling,* melt the fudge or nougat by putting it into a small pot with a handle. Carefully place the pot in a bigger pot partially filled with hot water.

10. *For vanilla filling,* add prepared pudding to the softened butter and mix until smooth and creamy.

11. Turn half of the baked

circles over. Cover their bottoms with either the fudge/nougat or the vanilla filling.

12. *To garnish,* knead the marzipan and the confectioners' sugar together. Divide it into five portions.

13. Dye one portion yellow, one green, one red, and one lilac

(use a little red and blue coloring together). Leave one portion white. Work the color through the marzipan.

14. From the red marzipan, shape the flat tongues and place them onto the fillings.

15. *For the icing*, put ¾ cup of confectioners' sugar in a small bowl. Add the lemon juice and stir until smooth. (If more icing is wanted, double the amounts.) Separate the icing into portions. Use food coloring to dye the icing any color you like.

16. Spread icing over the tops of the cookies without filling. Place them on top of the filled cookies to form the heads.

17. Make the hair by squeezing pieces of marzipan through a garlic press.

18. Flatten some marzipan and cut out strips to form bows.

19. To make the eyes and noses, mold small balls. Cut them in half, and fix them onto each face.

20. To make a hat, shape two long pencil-thick rolls and attach them to the top of a head.

21. To finish the eyes, squirt on pupils with brown decorating gel. Use it to trim the hat too.

Have Ready

parchment paper
baking sheet
1 small glass
1 pencil
1 mixing bowl
1 electric mixer
1 rubber scraper
1 sifter
1 pastry bag
1 metal spatula
1 cake rack
1 small *and*

1 large pot (with handles)
1 small knife
1 garlic press

Giant Funny Faces

(6 portions)

What You Need

For the Dough

2 extra-large egg whites
½ cup sugar (125 g)
¼ t vanilla flavoring
1 cup all-purpose flour
   (100 g)
2 T cornstarch (30 g)
½ t baking powder
2 extra-large egg yolks

For the Filling

4 oz nutted fudge or nougat
   (100 g)
3½ oz cherry preserves
   (100 g)

For the Garnish

6½ oz white marzipan paste
   (200 g)
¾ cup confectioners' sugar
   (100 g)
food coloring
decorating gel

How It's Done

1. Put parchment paper on the baking sheet. Use two glasses, one larger than the other, to draw circles on the paper. Draw 3 small circles and 1 larger one, for each Giant Funny Face.

2. *To make the dough and bake,* follow the directions on page 8 for Funny Faces (steps 2–7).

3. *For the filling,* melt the fudge or nougat by putting it in a small pot with a handle. Carefully place it in a bigger pot partially filled with hot water.

4. *For the garnish,* knead the sifted confectioners' sugar into the marzipan. Separate it into three portions. With food coloring, dye one portion green and another red. Put them aside.

5. For each Giant Funny Face, spread preserves on one small baked circle and melted fudge or nougat on another.

6. Take the green marzipan and mold it into a ruff. Fasten this collar onto the third small circle. Use some jelly, icing, or decorating gel as a sticky "glue."

7. Take the red and the white marzipan and mold the eyes, nose, mouth, and hat of the Giant Funny Faces (see instructions for Funny Faces on pages 8–9). Stick them onto the bigger, baked circles to make the faces. Put the 4 circles together to build the Giant Funny Faces.

Have Ready

parchment paper
baking sheet
1 glass, about 2 inches
   (5 cm) diameter
1 glass, about 2¼ inches
   (6 cm) diameter
1 pencil
1 mixing bowl
1 electric mixer
1 pastry bag
1 metal spatula
1 cake rack
1 small *and*
1 large pot (with handles)
1 pastry brush

Dragon's Volcano Cake

What You Need

For the Dough

8 T butter, softened (125 g)
6½ T sugar (100 g)
2 t vanilla sugar (10 g)
1 T grated lemon peel
2 eggs
½ cup plus 1½ T all-purpose
    flour (75 g)
3 T cornstarch (50 g)
1 t baking powder
3 T ground almonds (30 g)
breadcrumbs

For the Filling

7 T butter, softened (100 g)
1 cup prepared pudding,
    vanilla

For the Garnish

1 pkg cake frosting, light
decorating gel
sugar flowers
8 oz white marzipan paste
    (200 g)
food coloring
pastry decorations
1 T chopped almonds
3 T confectioners' sugar
    (50 g)

How It's Done

1. *For the dough,* beat the butter smooth while sprinkling the sugar and vanilla sugar in slowly.

2. Mix in the grated lemon peel. One by one, crack open and stir in the eggs.

3. Put the flour in a small bowl. Add the cornstarch and baking powder. Mix it well.

4. Sift the flour into the butter-egg mixture a little at a time, stirring it in. Last, add and mix in the ground almonds.

5. Grease a small tube or bundt cake pan, about 6 inches (16 cm) diameter, using butter or shortening. Line the greased pan with breadcrumbs.

6. Pour or spoon the dough into the pan. Slide the pan onto the middle rack of a *pre-heated* oven.

**Oven setting:
about 350°F (175°C)**

**Baking time:
45–50 minutes**

7. Remove the cake from the oven. When it has cooled a little, take the cake out of the pan and let it cool completely on a cake rack. Use a cake cutter to cut the cooled cake horizontally into two halves.

8. *For the filling,* spoon the softened butter into the vanilla pudding and blend it thoroughly.

9. Spread half of the filling on the lower layer of the cake and replace the top part. Put the remaining filling in a bowl to serve on the side.

10. *For the icing,* prepare the cake frosting, following the directions on the package. Spread it evenly over the cake.

11. *For the garnish,* decorate the cake with colorful gel and sugar flowers.

12. *To make the dragon,* knead the marzipan paste with the sifted confectioners' sugar until it is smooth.

13. Break off some marzi-

pan. Mold two small balls to make the eyes. Dye another piece of marzipan red with food coloring. Use it to make the baby dragon's tongue.

14. Take another piece of marzipan. Make the hair by mixing red and green food coloring (it makes brown) and squeezing it through a garlic press.

15. Knead the remaining marzipan with green food coloring. Mold the dragon's body and the ridge down its back.

16. Using marmalade or icing, "glue" the eyes, hair

and tongue onto the dragon. Put pastry decorations on as nostrils. Press chopped almonds onto the body to

give the dragon some scales.

17. Finally, squirt pupils onto the marzipan eyes and paint the dragon's toes with decorating gel.

Have Ready

1 mixing bowl
1 wooden spoon *or*
1 electric mixer
1 flour sifter
1 spatula
1 tube or bundt cake pan, 6 inches (16 cm) diameter
1 cake rack
1 small *and*
1 larger pot (with handles)
1 pastry brush
1 garlic press

Fiesta Mountains *(12 portions)*

What You Need

For Dough and Filling

4 eggs
½ cup sugar (125 g)
2 t vanilla sugar
½ t grated lemon peel
2 T cornstarch (30 g)
2 pinches baking powder
¾ cup plus 1 T all-purpose
    flour (100 g)
butter (to grease tin)
3 oz nutted fudge/nougat
    (100 g)

For the Icing

4 oz semi-sweet chocolate
    (125 g)
2 T solid white shortening,
or
2 T lemon juice
¾ cup confectioners' sugar
    (125 g)

For the Garnish

candy sprinkles
decorating gel
sugar flowers
pastry decorations
chocolate hearts

How It's Done

1. *For the dough,* break the eggs and put them in a mixing bowl. Whip them until frothy, adding sugar, vanilla sugar and lemon peel slowly.

2. Mix the cornstarch and baking powder into the flour. Sift them onto the egg mixture while stirring them in slowly.

3. Grease the tin thoroughly and fill the pockets 2/3 full with the dough batter.

4. Place the tin on a baking sheet and slide it into the *pre-heated* oven.

**Oven setting:
400°F (200°C)**

**Baking time:
about 15 minutes**

5. Take the baked cakes out of the tin. Let them cool on a cake rack.

6. With round side up, slice them across 2/3 of the way down.

7. *For the filling,* place the fudge or nougat in a small pot with a handle. Carefully place this pot in a larger pot partially filled with hot water. Let the candy melt.

8. Spread the filling on the lower portions of the cakes. Replace the tops.

9. *For the chocolate icing,* melt the chocolate in a pot placed in hot water (like you did the filling). Remove it

from the heat. Add the shortening and stir until smooth. Let the icing cool.

10. *For the white icing,* add lemon juice to the confectioners' sugar. Stir the icing until smooth and ready to spread.

11. Frost half of the cookies with the chocolate icing. Cover the other half with the lemon icing.

12. Decorate the cookies using sprinkles, decorating gel, sugar flowers, candy-coated chocolate bits, pastry decorations, and chocolate hearts.

Have Ready

1 mixing bowl
1 wooden spoon *or*
1 electric mixer
1 round-bottomed muffin tin
    (see Tip 1)
1 rubber scraper
1 baking sheet
1 cake rack
2 small *and*
2 larger pots (with handles)
1 pastry brush

Tips

1. Find round-bottomed tins in specialty stores or make muffin cups by molding foil around a ball.

2. Frost cookies with both icings to make Half 'n' Halfs.

Chocolated Fruits

What You Need

grapes
orange slices
peeled, steamed apples,
    sliced
small pears, quartered
rhubarb pieces
strawberries
candied fruits
herb leaves
1 pkg chocolate coating, *or*
1 bar of milk, dark, *or*
semi-sweet chocolate

How It's Done

1. Place the washed or steamed fruits on a paper towel. Dab them dry.

2. Prepare the coating, following directions on the package, *or*

3. Cut the chocolate into pieces and put them in a small pot. Place this pot in a bigger pot partly filled with hot water. Let the chocolate melt.

4. Using toothpicks, pick up and dip the fruits one by one into the chocolate. Place them carefully on a rack to dry.

5. To prepare them for gift-giving, arrange the chocolated fruits in a glass, porcelain bowl, or a pretty box lined with grease-proof paper. Cover it with cellophane paper and tie it with ribbon, making a pretty bow.

Have Ready

paper towel
1 knife
1 small *and*
1 larger pot (with handles)
toothpicks
1 cake rack

Sad Sack Clown

What You Need

For the Dough

2 sticks butter, softened
   (250 g)
1 cup sugar (250 g)
4 t vanilla sugar
4 eggs
1 pinch salt
3¼ cups all-purpose flour
   (400 g)
3 T baking powder
½ cup milk (125 mL)

For the Icing

¾ cup confectioners' sugar
   (125 g)
2 T lemon juice
food coloring

For the Garnish

pastry decorations
decorating gel
paper curling ribbon
small balloons
construction paper

How It's Done

1. *For the dough*, stir the softened butter until smooth. One after the other, add the sugar, vanilla sugar, eggs, and salt. Stir it all together well.

2. In a bowl, mix the flour and baking powder. Sift the flour little by little into the butter batter. At the same time, add milk with a tablespoon and blend all together until smooth.

3. Pour or spoon the dough into a greased, man-shaped or clown figure baking tin. Slide the tin into the *pre-heated* oven.

**Oven setting:
350–400°F (175–200°C)**

**Baking time:
about 1 hour**

4. Move the baked figure to a cake rack to cool.

5. *For the icing*, put the confectioners' sugar in a bowl. Add the lemon juice and stir.

6. Divide the icing into portions. Dye them with food coloring.

7. Use the pastry brush to frost the cake. Follow the example in the photo, or "color" your own clown with the icing.

8. *Garnish it* with decorating gel and pastry decorations. Stick curling ribbon to the right and left of the hat as hair.

9. Out of construction paper, cut out a bowtie and big shoes for the clown. Stick them on with decorating gel or some icing.

Have Ready

2 mixing bowls
1 wooden spoon *or*
1 electric mixer
1 flour sifter
1 tablespoon
1 baking tin, man *or* clown shaped, greased
1 cake rack
1 small bowl
1 pastry brush
scissors

Little Lambs

What You Need

For the Dough

1 stick butter, softened
   (125 g)
½ cup sugar (125 g)
2 T vanilla sugar
¼ t vanilla flavoring
1 pinch salt
2 eggs
1 cup all-purpose flour
   (125 g)
breadcrumbs

For the Icing and Garnish

For white lamb:
1 cup confectioners' sugar
   (150 g)
1–2 T hot water
¼ cup shredded coconut
   (30 g)

For black lamb:
1 pkg dark chocolate icing
chocolate sprinkles

ribbon
small bells

How It's Done

1. *For the dough,* stir the softened butter until smooth. Slowly add the sugar and vanilla sugar and stir them in.

2. Add the vanilla flavoring and salt. Add the eggs and stir them in one by one.

3. Grease a lamb-shaped tin and line it with the bread-crumbs. Pour or spoon the batter into the tin. Slide the tin onto the middle rack of the *pre-heated* oven.

**Oven setting:
350–400°F (175–200°C)**

**Baking time:
35–45 minutes**

4. Remove the baked lamb from the tin. Let it cool on the cake rack.

5. *To frost the light lamb,* sift the confectioners' sugar into a small bowl. Add the hot water and stir it until the icing is thick but smooth.

6. Spread it evenly on the cooled cake. Sprinkle the frosted cake with shredded coconut.

7. *To frost the dark lamb,* coat it evenly with the chocolate frosting. Sprinkle the frosted lamb with chocolate sprinkles.

8. With a ribbon, tie on a little bell and make a bow around the lamb's neck.

Have Ready

1 mixing bowl
1 flour sifter
1 wooden spoon *or*
1 electric mixer
1 lamb tin, about 3 cups
  (750 mL) volume
1 cake rack
1 small pot
1 pastry brush

Baker Bunny and Egg Nests

(6 portions)

What You Need

For the Dough

3 cups whole wheat flour
1 pkg dry baking yeast
1 t salt
3 T butter, melted and
   cooled
7 T lukewarm milk
   (200 mL)
1 egg yolk
1–2 T milk

For the Garnish

¾ cup confectioners' sugar
   (125 g)
2 T lemon juice
food coloring
decorating gel
candy eggs
dyed/decorated hard-boiled
   eggs

How It's Done

1. *To make the dough*, place the flour in a bowl. Add the yeast and mix it together thoroughly.

2. Add salt, butter, and milk. Using the electric mixer with kneading hooks, blend the ingredients well.

3. Take the dough off the hooks. Put it on a table. If sticky, use a pastry scraper. Knead it with your hands into a smooth dough.

4. Let the dough sit at room temperature until you can see that it has "risen" (gotten bigger).

5. Roll the dough out to about ½ inch (1 cm) thick.

6. Trace the Baker Bunny on this page. Cut out the outline and put it on top of the rolled-out dough as a stencil. Cut out the figure.

7. Place the Baker Bunny on a baking sheet lined with parchment paper. From the extra dough, mold a little basket and hang it on the bunny's arm.

8. Divide the remaining

dough into 6 pieces and make rolls of about 20 inches (50 cm) long each. Cut the rolls into 2 halves.

9. Wind 2 pieces around each other. Shape them into wreaths and place them on the baking sheet.

10. In a cup or small bowl, mix the egg yolk with a little milk. Use a pastry brush to coat the baker and the wreaths with the mixture.

11. Let the figures sit on the baking sheet in a warm spot to "rise." When the dough has gotten bigger, slide the baking sheet into the *pre-heated* oven.

**Oven setting:
350–400°F (175–200°C)**

**Baking time:
15–20 minutes**

12. With a metal spatula, lift the baked figures from the baking sheet. Place them carefully on a cake rack to cool.

13. *For the icing*, put the confectioners' sugar in a small bowl. Add the lemon juice and mix until thick but smooth.

14. Separate the icing into portions. Dye the icing two or three colors with food coloring. Use a pastry brush to "paint" a shirt and pants onto the figure.

15. *To garnish*, trim the Baker Bunny with decorating gel. Make a baker's hat out of a piece of napkin. Stick it onto the bunny's head with some icing.

16. *To make the egg nests*, carefully press the cooked and decorated eggs into the middle of each of the wreaths.

Have Ready

1 mixing bowl
1 electric mixer (with kneading hooks)
1 pastry scraper
1 pencil
scissors
1 knife
1 baking sheet
parchment paper
1 cake rack
2–3 small bowls
1 pastry brush
1 napkin

Sweet Hearts

What You Need

For the Dough

2 cups all-purpose flour (250 g)
1 t baking powder
6½ T sugar (100 g)
2 t vanilla sugar
1 pinch salt
11 T butter, softened (175 g)
6½ T ground almonds (75 g)

For the Frosting and Garnish

1½ cup confectioners' sugar (250 g)
4 T lemon juice
food coloring
sugar flowers
decorating gel
pastry decorations

How It's Done

1. *For the dough*, mix the flour and baking powder and sift it into a bowl.

2. Add sugar, vanilla sugar, salt, butter, and chopped almonds. Blend all ingredients together well with an electric mixer, using the kneading attachment.

3. Take the dough off of the kneading hooks. Place it on a table. Using a pastry scraper, work it with your hands kneading the dough smooth. Put it in the refrigerator for about ½ hour.

4. Make a stencil for the big heart by placing tracing paper over the heart on the next page. Draw the outlines and cut out the stencil.

5. Put the dough on the table and roll it out to about ½ inch (1 cm) thick.

6. Put the stencil on top and cut out the heart. Put the dough scraps together and roll the dough out again to about ¼ inch (½ cm) thick for the smaller hearts.

7. Cut out the little hearts using a stencil you have made, small cookie cutters, or cut them out freehand. Place the hearts on a baking sheet covered with parchment paper. Slide the sheet onto the middle rack of the *pre-heated* oven.

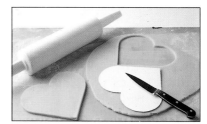

Oven setting:
350–400°F (175–200°C)

Baking time:
10–15 minutes
Note: The smaller cookies will bake faster than the larger ones.

8. With a metal spatula, take the golden-brown cookies off of the baking sheet and put them on a cake rack to cool.

9. *For the icing*, put the confectioners' sugar into a small bowl. Stir in the lemon juice until the icing is smooth and ready to spread.

10. Divide the icing into small portions. Dye them different colors with the food coloring. Cover the hearts with icing.

11. *To garnish*, trim the hearts with sugar flowers, decorating gel, and pastry decorations.

Have Ready

1 mixing bowl
1 flour sifter
1 electric mixer (with
   kneading hooks)
1 pastry scraper
tracing paper and pencil
scissors
1 rolling pin
1 knife
small cookie cutters
1 baking sheet
parchment paper
1 spatula
1 cake rack
1 small bowl

Laughing Strawberry Tarts

What You Need

For the Dough

5 T butter, softened (75 g)
   or 4 T (60 g)
5 T sugar (75 g) *or* ¼ cup
   (60 g)
1 t vanilla sugar
2 eggs
1 pinch salt
1¼ cups all-purpose flour
   (150 g) *or* 1 cup (120 g)
1 t baking powder
2 T milk

For the Topping and to Decorate

3 cups strawberries
3 T sugar
1 pkg red fruit glaze
1 heaping T sugar
whipped cream
candy sprinkles
pastry decorations
decorating gel

How It's Done

1. *For the dough*, beat the butter smooth. One after the other, add the sugar, vanilla sugar, eggs, and salt.

2. Mix the flour and baking powder. Little by little, sift the flour into the butter batter, alternating with spoonsful of milk. Use only as much milk as you need to make the dough drop off the spoon like a thick glue.

3. Spoon the dough into tart tins. Place the tins on the oven rack or a baking sheet and push them into the *pre-heated* oven.

**Oven setting:
350–400°F (175–200°C)**

**Baking time:
20–25 minutes**

4. Take the baked tarts out of the oven. Remove them from the tins and let them cool on a cake rack.

5. *To make the topping*, remove the stems and rinse off the strawberries. Let them drain well.

6. Sprinkle the strawberries with sugar and let them sit awhile. When the sugar has drawn a good amount of juice from the fruit, remove the berries and place them evenly in the tarts.

7. Take a cup (250 mL) of the strawberry juice (if necessary add water). Prepare a glaze with the measured juice, the tablespoon of sugar, and the contents of the red fruit glaze powder. Follow the directions on the package. Spread it evenly over the strawberries and let it harden.

8. *To decorate*, put the whipped cream into a pastry bag with just a hole at the tip. Squeeze out a stream of cream to make the curly hair, eyes, nose, and mouth on each of the tarts.

9. Adds dots of color to the eyes with decorating gel. Finish with candy sprinkles.

Have Ready

1 bowl
1 wooden spoon *or*
1 electric mixer
1 flour sifter
tart tins
1 cake rack
1 knife
1 pastry bag with hole in tip

Black-and-Whites

What You Need

For the Dough

6½ T butter, softened
  (100 g)
6½ T sugar (100 g)
2 t vanilla sugar
2 eggs
1 pinch salt
1 pkg instant pudding mix,
  vanilla
3 T milk
2 cups all-purpose flour
  (250 g)
1 T baking powder

For the Frosting

1 pkg frosting, vanilla
1 pkg frosting, chocolate

For the Garnish

pastry decorations
decorating gel
sugar flowers
candied cherries

How It's Done

1. *To make the dough*, beat the butter smooth. Add the sugar, vanilla sugar, eggs, and salt. Mix well. Stir in the instant pudding powder and the milk.

2. Mix the flour and baking powder. Sift it into the butter batter a little at a time and stir it in.

3. With the help of 2 tablespoons, take and roll small portions of dough from spoon to spoon. Drop the balls of dough onto a greased cookie sheet.

4. Carefully slide it into the *pre-heated* oven.

Oven setting:
350–400°F (175–200°C)

Baking time:
15–20 minutes

5. Remove the baked cookies from the sheet. Let them cool on a cake rack.

6. *For the frosting*, open and follow the instructions on the packages of prepared icing. Cover half of the cookies with the chocolate icing, and half with vanilla frosting.

7. *Garnish the cookies* with cake decoration, sugar flowers, and candied cherries. You can also draw designs or faces on them with decorating gel.

Have Ready

1 mixing bowl
1 wooden spoon *or*
1 electric mixer
2 tablespoons
1 cookie sheet
1 cake rack
1 pastry brush

Hedgehog Family

What You Need

For the Dough

4 oz butter, softened (125 g)
⅓ cup sugar (75 g)
2 t vanilla sugar
3 eggs
1 pinch salt
⅓ cup ground hazelnuts
   (75 g)
½ cup grated chocolate
   (100 g)
⅓ cup all-purpose flour
   (75 g)
3 T cornstarch
2 t baking powder
1 T cocoa powder

For the Icing

4 oz semi-sweet chocolate
   (125 g)
3 T solid white shortening

For the Garnish

¼ cup slivered almonds
   (50 g)
raisins

How It's Done

1. *For the dough*, beat the butter smooth while slowly adding in sugar and vanilla sugar.

2. One after the other, stir in the eggs, hazelnuts, and the grated chocolate.

3. Mix the flour, baking powder, cornstarch, and cocoa. Sift it onto the butter batter a little at a time, stirring it in.

4. When all the flour is moistened, spoon the dough into one large and five small, greased hedgehog tins.

5. Place the tins on the middle rack of the *preheated* oven, and carefully slide them in.

Oven setting:
300–350°F (150–175°C)

Baking time:
1 hour (large cake)
30 minutes (small cakes)

6. Using oven mitts, take the tins from the oven. When the cakes have cooled slightly, remove them from the tins. Let them cool completely on a cake rack.

7. *For the icing*, put the chocolate into a small pot with a handle. Place the pot in a bigger pot partially filled with hot water to melt the chocolate.

8. Cover the hedgehog shapes completely with the melted chocolate.

9. *To garnish*, press in raisins (or currants) for the eyes. Poke holes in the hedgehog cakes with a toothpick. Push in slivered almonds for the quills.

Have Ready

1 mixing bowl
1 wooden spoon *or*
1 electric mixer
1 flour sifter
1 rubber scraper
hedgehog tins
1 small *and*
1 larger pot (with handles)
1 cake rack
1 pastry brush
toothpicks

Quick Choco-Orange Cupcakes *(about 16 portions)*

What You Need

For the Dough

1 pkg orange cake mix
4 oz butter, softened (125 g)
2 eggs
water

For the Garnish

1 pkg chocolate frosting
sugar flowers
candy sprinkles
pastry decorations
decorating gel

How It's Done

1. *For the dough*, prepare the orange cake mix, adding butter, eggs, and water according to the directions on the package.

2. Place the bake cups in a muffin tin and spoon one heaping tablespoon of dough into each one. Place the tin in the *pre-heated* oven.

Oven setting:
350°F (175°C)

Baking time:
about 30 minutes

3. Place the tin on a cake rack. When cool, remove the muffins from the tin.

4. *For the garnish*, place a heaping teaspoonful of chocolate frosting in the middle of each cupcake.

5. Finish the decorating with sugar flowers, sprinkles, pastry decorations, or decorating gel.

Have Ready

1 mixing bowl
1 wooden spoon *or*
1 electric mixer
1 rubber scraper
paper bake cups
1 muffin tin
1 cake rack
1 teaspoon

"My Place" Munchies

What You Need

For the Dough

2 cups all-purpose flour
   (250 g)
5 T sugar (75 g)
2 t vanilla sugar
1 pinch salt
1 egg
1 stick butter, softened
   (125 g)

For the Garnish

¾ cup confectioners' sugar
   (125 g)
2 T lemon juice
food coloring
decorating gel
pastry decoration

How It's Done

1. *For the dough*, sift the flour into a bowl. Add sugar, vanilla sugar, salt, egg, and butter. Blend everything together well with an electric mixer with kneading hooks.

2. Remove the dough from the hooks. Place it on the table and knead it by hand until the dough is smooth.

3. Let the dough rest, covered, for about an hour in the refrigerator.

4. Sprinkle a baking board or tabletop with flour. Put the dough on it and roll the dough out to about ¼ inch (½ cm) thick.

5. For stencils, trace the pictures of the car, airplane, and ship in this book. You can also use pictures from books or magazines, or make up your own. Cut out the stencils.

6. Place the stencils on the dough. Cut out the dough figures. Place them on a cookie sheet covered with parchment paper.

7. Use up the remaining dough by cutting out more cookie shapes and add them to the cookie sheet. Slide the sheet into the *pre-heated* oven.

**Oven setting:
350–400°F (175–200°C)**

**Baking time:
about 15 minutes**

8. *For the icing*, put the confectioners' sugar in a small bowl. Add the lemon juice and mix until thick but smooth.

9. Divide the icing into 4 or 5 portions. Leave one white. Color the other portions with food coloring.

10. Use a pastry brush to "color" the cookies. Look at the cookies shown here as a guide.

11. *Garnish the cookies* with sugar flowers and pastry decorations. For use as party place cards, write the names of the guests on the cookies with decorating gel.

Have Ready

1 mixing bowl
1 flour sifter
1 electric mixer
  (with knead-
  ing hooks)
1 rolling pin
cookie cutters
1 cookie sheet
parchment paper
1 cake rack
1 pastry brush
4 small bowls

Pretty Little House

What You Need

For the Dough

2 sticks butter, softened
    (250 g)
½ cup sugar (125 g)
1 T vanilla sugar
3 extra large eggs
1 egg yolk
1 pinch salt
1 T grated orange *or* lemon
    peel
1½ cups all-purpose flour
    (190 g)
2 T cornstarch
1¼ t baking powder
2 T orange liqueur *or* 2 T
    lemon juice
⅓ cup chopped almonds
    (50 g)
breadcrumbs

For the Garnish

¾ cup confectioners' sugar
    (125 g)
2 T lemon juice
sugar flowers
pastry decorations
food coloring
decorating gel
1–2 T confectioners' sugar
some egg white

How It's Done

1. *For the dough*, work the
butter adding sugar and
vanilla sugar slowly. Blend it
together until smooth.

2. Stir in the three eggs, the
extra egg yolk, salt, and
either the grated orange or
lemon peel.

3. Mix the flour, cornstarch
and baking powder. Sift it
into the butter batter a little
at a time and stir it in.

4. Add and stir in the orange liqueur or lemon juice
and the shredded almonds.

5. Pour or spoon the dough
into a well-greased tin
(shaped like a house) lined
with breadcrumbs.

6. Slide the tin onto the
middle rack of the *pre-
heated* oven.

**Oven setting:
300–350°F (150–175°C)**

**Baking time:
about 65 minutes**

7. Let the baked cake cool
in the tin for about 10 minutes. Turn it out onto the
cake rack to cool completely.

8. *For the icing*, put the
confectioners' sugar in a
small bowl. Add the lemon
juice and mix until smooth.

9. Cover the roof and lower
part of the house with the
icing. Add white sugar sprinkles to the "snow."

10. Decorate the whole
house with pastry decora-
tions, sugar flowers, small
candies, and decorative gel.

11. Mix confectioners' sugar
and egg white until smooth
to make "frozen" white ici-
cles that cling to the roof.

Have Ready

1 mixing bowl
1 wooden spoon *or*
1 electric mixer
1 flour sifter
1 rubber
    scraper
1 house-
    shaped tin
1 cake rack

Roly-Poly Snowman

What You Need

For the Dough

¼ cup honey (100 g)
3 T sugar (50 g)
1 pinch salt
1½ T butter, softened (25 g)
1 T water
1 egg
½ t ground cinnamon
2 drops almond flavoring
2 cups all-purpose flour
   (250 g)
1 oz cocoa powder (25 g)
1 T baking powder

For the Frosting and to Garnish

½ cup confectioners' sugar
   (100 g)
egg white
pastry decoration
small colorful candies
red jellybean

How It's Done

1. *For the dough*, put the honey, sugar, salt, butter, and water into a pot. Heat it up slowly while stirring with a wooden spoon.

2. Pour the honey mixture into a big bowl and let it cool. When the mix is almost cold, stir in the egg and the spices.

3. Mix the flour, baking powder, and cocoa together. Sift about one-half of the flour, a little at a time, into the honey mixture, mixing it in.

4. Place the dough on a table. Little by little, sift the remaining flour onto the dough. Knead it in by hand.

5. Roll the dough out to about ½ inch (1 cm) thick.

6. With tracing paper, copy the outline of the snowman illustrated here. Cut it out and use it to cut a snow person out of the dough.

7. Place the figure on a well-greased cookie sheet. Slide it onto the middle rack of the *pre-heated* oven.

**Oven setting:
350–400°F (175–180°C)**

**Baking time:
about 10 minutes**

8. When the figure is baked light brown, remove it from the oven. Using a metal spatula, slide it from the sheet to a cake rack to cool.

9. *For the frosting*, mix the confectioners' sugar and the egg white into a thick, sticky glaze. Use a pastry brush and cover the front of the snowman completely.

10. *Garnish the figure* with pastry decorations and candies. Cut a red jelly bean into strips and stick it on with icing to make a mouth.

Have Ready

1 pot
1 mixing bowl
1 wooden spoon
1 knife
1 cookie sheet
1 cake rack
1 small bowl
1 teaspoon
1 pastry brush

Heavenly Horse and Sun, Moon and Stars

What You Need

For the Dough

⅓ cup honey (125 g)
1 T confectioners' sugar
2 t vanilla sugar
1 egg
2 cups all-purpose flour
  (250 g)
1 t baking powder
1 T evaporated milk

For the Garnish

¾ cup confectioners' sugar
  (125 g)
2 T lemon juice
food coloring
decorating gel
granulated sugar
orange marmalade
confectioners' sugar

How It's Done

1. *For the dough,* put the honey in a small bowl. Sift in the confectioners' sugar. Add and mix in the vanilla sugar and egg with a wooden spoon.

2. In another bowl, mix the flour and baking powder. Sift about two-thirds of it into the honey mix.

3. Take the dough out of the bowl and place it on a table. Work it by hand, sifting and kneading the remaining flour into it.

4. Roll out the dough to about ½ inch (1 cm) thick. Place tracing paper on the horse illustrated here and copy the outline.

5. Cut out a stencil. Place it on the dough and cut out the horse. Also cut out 2 little squares to make the packages.

6. Roll out the remaining dough to about ¼ inch (½ cm) thick and punch out stars, moons, circles and wreaths with cookie cutters.

7. Place the horse and the other shapes on a baking sheet covered with parchment paper. Brush evaporated milk on the figures.

8. Slide the baking sheet onto the middle rack of the *pre-heated* oven.

**Oven setting:
350–400°F (175–200°C)**

**Baking time:
15–20 minutes**
Note: The smaller cookies will bake faster than the large ones.

9. Remove the baked cookies from the sheet. Place them carefully on a cake rack to cool.

10. *For the icing,* put the confectioners' sugar in a small bowl. Add and stir in lemon juice a little at a time until the icing is slightly thick but smooth.

11. Divide the sugar icing into 3 or 4 portions. Dye them different colors with the food coloring.

12. Using the pastry brush, coat the horse and the little packages with the colored icing. Coat the horse's mane with a light-colored icing or decorating gel.

13. *To garnish,* trim the horse with decorating gel and sprinkle the lower part with confectioners' sugar.

14. Coat the moons with light-colored sugar icing and sprinkle the stars with hail or granulated sugar.

15. For the suns, coat the baked circles with orange marmalade. Sprinkle confectioners' sugar on the pastry wreaths. Place them on the orange-marmalade-coated cookies.

Have Ready

2 mixing bowls
1 flour sifter
1 wooden spoon
1 rolling pin
1 pencil
tracing paper
scissors
small cookie cutters
1 baking sheet

parchment
  paper
1 cake rack
1 tablespoon
3-4 small bowls
1 pastry brush

39

Decorated Fir Trees *(4 large and 7–10 small trees)*

What You Need

For the Dough

1¼ cups all-purpose flour
   (300 g)
1 t baking powder
3 T sugar (50 g)
3 egg yolks
11 T butter, softened (175 g)

For the Garnish

2–3 T orange marmalade
3 egg whites
⅔ cup sugar (150 g)
½ t ground cinnamon
1¼ cups shredded coconut
   (150 g)
pastry decorations
decorating gel
sugar icing

How It's Done

1. *For the dough,* mix the flour and the baking powder. Sift it into a bowl.

2. Add sugar, the egg yolk, and butter. Mix the ingredients well with an electric mixer with kneading hooks.

3. Take the dough from the hooks. Put it on a table and knead it with your hands until it is smooth.

4. Put the dough in the refrigerator and let it sit for 1 hour.

5. With tracing paper, copy the outline of the large tree in the picture. Cut out a stencil.

6. Roll the dough out to about ¼ inch (½ cm) thick. Lay the tree stencil on the dough and cut out 4 fir trees.

7. To make other fir trees, use small cookie cutters, make a smaller stencil, or cut the cookies out freehand.

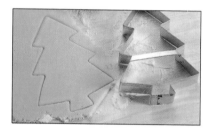

8. Place the trees on a well-greased cookie sheet. Place it on the middle rack in the *pre-heated* oven.

**Oven setting:
400°F (200°C)**

**Baking time:
about 10 minutes**

9. As the cookies bake, strain orange marmalade through a small sieve.

10. Take the baked cookies out of the oven. Brush them with the orange jam.

11. *To frost the trees,* use a

whisk to beat the egg whites with sugar and cinnamon until stiff. Carefully fold in the shredded coconut. Coat the tree branches with this mixture.

12. Slide the cookie sheet back into the heated oven.

**Oven setting:
275–300°F (130–150°C)**

**Baking time:
20–25 minutes**

13. Remove the baked trees from the oven. With a metal spatula, lift them from the cookie sheet and put them on a cake rack to cool.

14. *Garnish the white-frosted trees* with pastry decorations and decorating gel or touches of colored sugar icing.

Have Ready

1 mixing bowl
1 flour sifter
1 electric mixer (with
   kneading hooks)
tracing paper
pencil
scissors
1 rolling pin
1 knife
small cookie cutters
1 cookie sheet, greased
1 small sieve
1 pastry brush
1 small bowl
1 wire whisk
1 cake rack

41

Santa's Boot

What You Need

For the Dough

¹⁄₃ cup honey (125 g)
3 T sugar (50 g)
2 t vanilla sugar
2 oz butter, softened (60 g)
1 egg yoke
2 pinches ground cinnamon
2 pinches ground cloves
2 cups all-purpose flour
   (250 g)
1 t baking powder
1 t cocoa powder

For the Garnish

decorating gel
small candies (red and
   green)
almonds, blanched and
   halved
icing

How It's Done

1. *For the dough*, put the honey, sugar, vanilla sugar, and butter in a small pot. Heat it over low heat, stirring slowly, until it is melted.

2. Pour the melted ingredients into a bowl. Place it in the refrigerator to cool quickly.

3. When the mixture is almost cold, stir in the egg yolk, cinnamon, and cloves.

4. In another bowl, mix and sift the flour with the baking powder and cocoa. Slowly stir two-thirds of it into the honey batter.

5. Put the dough on a table. Knead the remaining portion of the flour mix into it with your hands.

6. Roll the dough out to about ¼ inch (½ cm) thick.

7. Place tracing paper on the boot cookie shown here. Copy the outline and cut out a stencil.

8. Place the stencil on the dough and cut out the boot. Use the remaining dough to make cookies in other shapes.

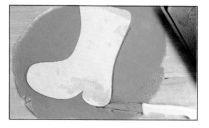

9. Place the boot and other cookies on a well-greased cookie sheet. Slide the sheet onto the middle rack in the *pre-heated* oven.

**Oven setting:
350–400°F
(175–200°C)**

**Baking time:
about 15 minutes**

10. Carefully remove the boot and cookies from the cookie sheet to a cake rack to cool.

11. *To garnish,* trim Santa's boot and the cookies with decorating gel, small candies, the half almonds, and extra icing.

Have Ready

1 pot
1 wooden spoon
2 bowls
1 flour sifter
1 rolling pin
1 knife
cookie cutters
1 cookie sheet
1 cake rack

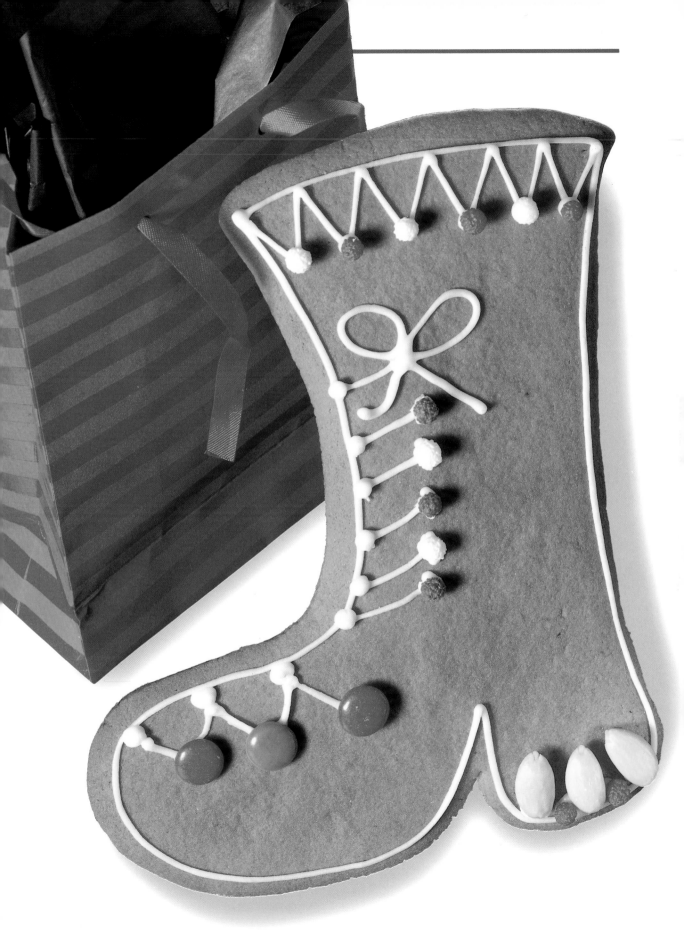

Marzipan Lucky Charms

(3 clover leaves, 3 little pigs, 4 ladybugs, 3 horseshoes)

What You Need

For the Dough

6½ oz fine marzipan paste (200 g)
⅔ cup confectioners' sugar, sifted (100 g)
food coloring
decorating gel
1 spaghetti strand, raw

How It's Done

1. Knead the marzipan paste with the sifted confectioners' sugar. Separate the marzipan into 4 portions.

2. Dye one part green, one part bright red, one part pink (a little bit of red coloring), and leave one part light.

3. *To make clover leaves*, roll out the green marzipan to about ¼ inch (½ cm) thick. Using a glass, cut out 3 circles about 2½ inches (6 cm) in diameter.

4. Make 4 small cuts into each marzipan circle. Round the edges a bit to make the cloverleaf shapes. Mold 3 green marzipan stems and press them onto each cloverleaf.

5. *To make the piglets*, roll out the pink marzipan.

Trace the piglets shown to make a stencil, punch out the piglets with cookie cutters, or cut them out freehand. Stick little cloverleafs, made out of remaining green marzipan, in the piglets' mouths.

6. *To make the ladybugs*, mold the red marzipan into 2 balls. Cut them in half to make 4 ladybug bodies.

7. Out of white marzipan, mold 6 legs for each ladybug. Press them onto the underside of the bodies so that they stick out at the sides.

8. Break the spaghetti strand into small pieces. Push them into the front of the ladybugs as "feelers." Finish the ladybugs with decorating gel.

9. *To make the horseshoes*, divide the white marzipan

into 3 portions. Make them into rolls about 7 inches long.

10. Shape the rolls into horseshoes, flattening them slightly. Put the horseshoe nails on them with decorating gel.

Have Ready

1 flour sifter
1 knife
3 small bowls
1 glass, about 2½ inches (6½ cm) diameter
1 rolling pin
pig cookie cutter
tracing paper
pencil

Sack o' Seasons Treat

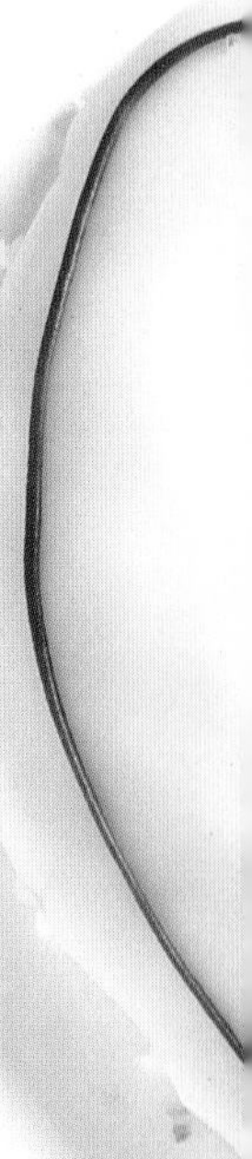

What You Need

For the Dough

1⅓ cups all-purpose flour
(150 g)
3 t baking powder
1½ oz low-fat cream cheese
(35 g)
1½ oz ricotta cheese (35 g)
3 T salad oil
3 T milk
2½ T sugar (35 g)
2½ t vanilla sugar (10 g)
1 pinch salt

For the Garnish

¾ cup confectioners' sugar
(125 g)
2 T lemon juice
food coloring
decorating gel
pastry decorations

How It's Done

1. *For the dough*, mix the flour and baking powder. Sift it into a bowl.

2. Add the cheeses, oil, milk, sugar, vanilla sugar, and salt. Blend all the ingredients together, using an electric mixer with kneading hooks, on high speed.

3. Roll the dough out to about ½ inch (1 cm) thick.

4. Place tracing or parchment paper on the cake shown here and copy the outline. Cut out a stencil. Place it on the dough and cut it out.

5. Place the cookie on a baking sheet lined with parchment paper. Slide the sheet onto the middle rack of the *pre-heated* oven.

Oven setting:
400°F (200°C)

Baking time:
about 12 minutes

6. With a metal spatula, remove the cookie from the baking sheet. Let it cool on a cake rack.

7. *For the icing*, put the confectioners' sugar in a small bowl. Add lemon juice and stir until the icing is thick but smooth.

8. Separate the icing into 5 portions. Leave one part white. With food coloring, dye one portion green, another yellow, the third red, and the last brown (use red and green together).

9. Coat the New Year sack with brown icing. Divide the upper part of the cookie into 4 sections. Frost one part green (for spring), one yellow (for summer), one red (for autumn), and one white (for winter).

10. *Garnish the sack* with colored sugar or sprinkles and pastry decorations. With decorating gel, write the names of the escaping seasons on this special New Year's treat.

Have Ready

1 flour sifter
1 mixing bowl
scissors
tracing paper
1 electric mixer (with kneading hooks)
1 rolling pin
1 baking sheet
parchment paper
1 cake rack
5 small bowls
1 pastry brush

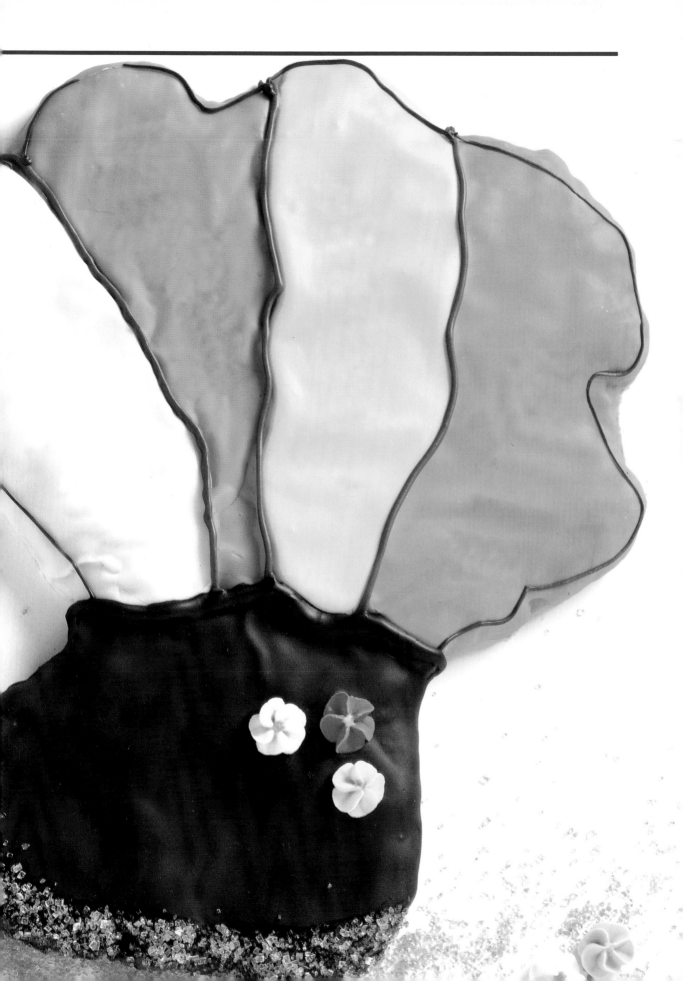

Index